The QUIZ BOOK ABOUT ME ... and you!

by H. Becker

Mexico City New Delhi Hong Kong Buenos Aires

Scholastic Canada Ltd.
604 King Street West, Toronto, Ontario M5V 1E1, Canada

Scholastic Inc.
557 Broadway, New York, NY 10012, USA

Scholastic Australia Pty Limited
PO Box 579, Gosford, NSW 2250, Australia

Scholastic New Zealand Limited
Private Bag 94407, Botany, Manukau 2163, New Zealand

Scholastic Children's Books
Euston House, 24 Eversholt Street, London NW1 1DB, UK

www.scholastic.ca

Library and Archives Canada Cataloguing in Publication

Becker, Helaine, 1961-, author
The quiz book about me ... and you / H. Becker.
ISBN 978-1-4431-4300-4 (pbk.)
1. Personality tests for children--Juvenile literature.
2. Child psychology--Miscellanea. 3. Personality--Juvenile
literature. 4. Individuality--Juvenile literature. I. Title.
BF697.B42 2015   j155.4   C2015-901892-7

Cover illustrations © iStockphoto.com: girls (AnjaRabenstein), pattern (aqabiz), doodles (dimonspace). Interior illustrations © by Shutterstock.com.

Text copyright © 2015 by Helaine Becker.

6 5 4 3 2 1   Printed in Canada 121   15 16 17 18 19

MIX
Paper from
responsible sources
FSC® C004071

Table of Contents

Introduction

What makes you tick? Are you an extrovert or an introvert? An ox or a monkey? A ruby or an amethyst? This insightful quiz book will give you a fascinating glimpse into the secret workings of your own mind and heart. What you discover will astound you, amaze you and make you laugh out loud! (P.S. Share these quizzes with your friends to find out what makes them tick too!)

Who Are You?

Check out the smiley face pictured here. What three words do you see FIRST? These best describe your personality.

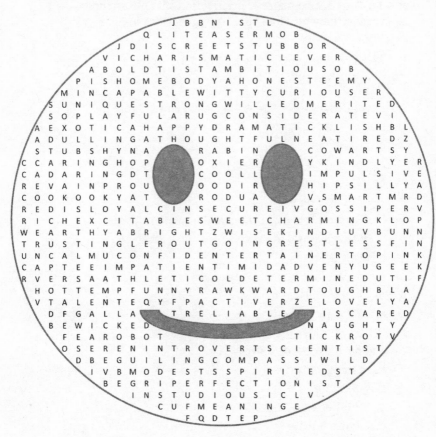

Take Five

Everyone's personality is unique, but psychologists have determined that your basic temperament can be described as a mixture of five major traits. These traits govern how you experience the world and your likely reactions in different everyday situations.

Answer each question by choosing which response most closely mirrors your feelings.

1. I consider myself to be enthusiastic and outgoing.
   a. Strongly disagree
   b. Disagree
   c. Neither agree nor disagree
   d. Agree a little
   e. Strongly agree
2. I am often critical of others and argumentative.
   a. Strongly disagree
   b. Disagree
   c. Neither agree nor disagree
   d. Agree a little
   e. Strongly agree
3. Others consider me to be reliable and have excellent self-control.
   a. Strongly disagree
   b. Disagree
   c. Neither agree nor disagree
   d. Agree a little
   e. Strongly agree

4. I tend to be anxious and get upset easily.
   a. Strongly disagree
   b. Disagree
   c. Neither agree nor disagree
   d. Agree a little
   e. Strongly agree

5. In general, I embrace new experiences and challenges.
   a. Strongly disagree
   b. Disagree
   c. Neither agree nor disagree
   d. Agree a little
   e. Strongly agree

6. In general, I tend to be quiet and reserved.
   a. Strongly disagree
   b. Disagree
   c. Neither agree nor disagree
   d. Agree a little
   e. Strongly agree

7. Others usually consider me to be warm-hearted and sympathetic.
   a. Strongly disagree
   b. Disagree
   c. Neither agree nor disagree
   d. Agree a little
   e. Strongly agree

8. I tend to be disorganized or careless in my daily work and habits.
   a. Strongly disagree
   b. Disagree

   c.   Neither agree nor disagree

   d.   Agree a little

   e.   Strongly agree

9.   In general, I tend to be calm, with an emotionally even keel.

   a.   Strongly disagree

   b.   Disagree

   c.   Neither agree nor disagree

   d.   Agree a little

   e.   Strongly agree

10. I consider myself to be fairly conventional and not particularly creative.

   a.   Strongly disagree

   b.   Disagree

   c.   Neither agree nor disagree

   d.   Agree a little

   e.   Strongly agree

Scoring

Look at the points below.

1.	a1	b2	c3	d4	e5
2.	a5	b4	c3	d2	e1
3.	a1	b2	c3	d4	e5
4.	a1	b2	c3	d4	e5
5.	a1	b2	c3	d4	e5
6.	a5	b4	c3	d2	e1
7.	a1	b2	c3	d4	e5
8.	a5	b4	c3	d2	e1
9.	a5	b4	c3	d2	e1
10.	a5	b4	c3	d2	e1

ADD together your points for questions 1 and 6. ___
ADD together your points for questions 2 and 7. ___
ADD together your points for questions 3 and 8. ___
ADD together your points for questions 4 and 9. ___
ADD together your points for questions 5 and 10. ___

How you rate . . .

Each pair of questions measures one of five major personality traits. Everyone has each trait in varying degrees. Here we used a scale of 2-10, with 2 being "very low" and 10 being "very high." Most people fall somewhere in the middle of each of these extremes. The combination of all five traits together gives us our unique personality profiles.

Extroversion — Questions 1 and 6

2-4 Happy hermit. You tend to feel more content and centred when you are either on your own or with a small group of family or friends that you know well. You enjoy the company of others, but too much hubbub leaves you feeling drained. Make sure to carve out quiet time for yourself every day!

5-7 Monkey in the middle. You are comfortable in a crowd, but also happy alone. You like a variety of experiences in your life, and to mix it up — today, a chill-out day on the sofa; tomorrow, a raucous get-together with your gal pals.

8-10 Social butterfly. "The more the merrier" is your motto, and people seek you out for your outgoing disposition. Extroverts can get restless and antsy when they spend too much time alone; they also can overwhelm their less outgoing sisters! Be sensitive to the needs of your less extroverted friends.

Agreeableness — Questions 2 and 7

2-4 Valiant porcupine. You tend to be very choosy about your friends. You can be prickly and will fight for something you believe is right even when everyone else disagrees with you.

5-7 Amiable otter. You value getting along with others but are happy to go it alone if following the crowd means going against your better judgment. People value your good sense and good manners.

8-10 Lovebird. Getting along with others is very important to you. You dislike conflict and will go to great lengths to make other people happy. Sometimes you put yourself last — don't let other people take advantage of your good nature!

Conscientiousness — Questions 3 and 8

2-4 Freewheeler. You tend to be lighthearted and spontaneous. These qualities are terrific, except when you, oops, forget your homework, again, and wind up in trouble for not doing your chores. "Live and let live" is your motto . . . or it would be if you could find it in that messy room of yours!

5-7 Steady Eddie. You are pretty good at following through — most of the time. But sometimes, you get distracted. All those games to play, books to read, movies to watch! No wonder you sometimes break your promises or skip your chores. Don't sweat it — but make a to-do list.

8-10 Laser beam. Your room is neat, your chores are done and of course you earned an A on your school project on the Mayans! You're the go-to gal when a task needs to be done and done right. Don't forget to kick back and have some fun too.

Emotional Stability — Questions 4 and 9

2-4 Ice cream sundae. You tend to be emotionally centred. Not much ruffles your feathers. Friends rely on you for keeping a cool head and dispensing good advice when they are confused or troubled. "Why sweat the small stuff?" is your motto.

5-7 Combo meal. Sure, you get down sometimes. And sure, sometimes you get so excited you just want to *SQUEEEEEE!* at the top of your lungs. But mostly, you're somewhere in the middle. Riding the waves, keeping things chill. Until, well, *SQUEEEEEE!*

8-10 Extra-spicy hot sauce. Can you say Drama Queen? Your emotions are like a yo-yo riding a roller coaster in a tsunami. You feel everything intensely and can go from utter despair to total ecstasy in .63 seconds. Your emotional range gives you the enviable ability to empathize with others. But it can also leave you exhausted from constantly pinging from one extreme to the other.

Openness to Experiences — Questions 5 and 10

2-4 Home bunny. You love your own space — your favourite old quilt on your bed, just like always. Your lunch, the same safe turkey on white you've favoured since grade one. And your old friends — you are loyal, loyal, loyal!

5-7 Rockin' robin. You like the safe and familiar. You find routines reassuring, because they keep your life easy-peasy. But you also enjoy novelty — trying laser tag, maybe, or checking out a sewing class with your bestie. You think variety is the spice of life — as long as you can be home by 10 and sleeping in your own bed.

8-10 High-flying condor. Today, you experiment with red streaks in your hair. Tomorrow? Plotting your future career as a spy or Arctic explorer. You are extremely curious, open-minded and eager to grab life by both ears and shake! You are probably a nonconformist, sensitive to art and music and very creative.

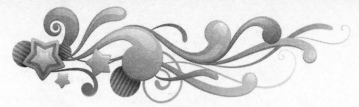

One of the Crowd or One in a Million?

Everyone likes to feel special. But it's also a great feeling to know you belong and have plenty in common with the people around you. Take this quiz to find out if you are reassuringly typical or refreshingly quirky!

1. Pick a number between 5 and 12. What is it?
2. Repeate the number 6 to yourself as fast as you can for 15 seconds. Go! Now think of a vegetable. What is it?
3. Think of a country that starts with D. What is it?
4. Now think of an animal that starts with the last letter of the country name you gave in question 3. What is it?
5. Now think of a fruit that starts with the last letter of the animal you came up with in question 4. What is it?
6. Think of a colour. What is it?
7. Think of a kind of tool. What is it?
8. Now some simple math! Start with 1000. Add 40. Add another 1000, then another 30. Add another 1000. Add 20. Add another 1000. Add 10.
   What is your answer?
9. Study this paragraph: FRieNDLy FLAKeS Are The Re-SULT OF DeCADeS OF SCIeNTIF-IC STUDY COMBINeD WITH CeNTURieS OF TASTe TrAInING

   How many Fs are in the paragraph?

Scoring

The most common answers given to these questions are listed below. Give yourself one point for each of your answers that mirrors the most typical response.

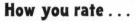

1. 7
2. Carrot
3. Denmark
4. Kangaroo
5. Orange
6. Red
7. Hammer
8. 5000 (The correct answer, though, is 4100!)
9. 3 (The correct answer, though, is 6!)

How you rate . . .

0-3 One in a million. Your mind works in mysterious ways. Because you think differently than other people, you are likely to have a very original life, full of invention and creativity!

4-7 One of a kind. You have much in common with the people around you, but you also tend to follow your own path and see things from a unique perspective. Your ability to connect with others — yet maintain your own viewpoint — will lead you toward exciting opportunities and rewarding friendships with interesting people.

8-9 One of us. You can relax — you are not strange. Well, not stranger than anyone else, anyway! Your very normal-ness gives you great powers of empathy — the ability to understand what others are thinking and feeling. This will make you a valued friend.

The Swirl

On a separate piece of paper, draw a quickie version of the shape below. Neatness doesn't count, so just draw it quickly, without thinking about it too much. Then turn the page to find out what your quickie pic reveals about you.

What your drawing says about you . . .

How you drew your quickie pic — not what it looks like — is what counts.

If you drew it from the inside out . . . you are somewhat conventional in the way you view the world: in general, you believe that what you see is what you get. You take people at face value and tend to be trusting and open-minded. You think the best way to understand any new topic is to start small and work your way up — the big picture will eventually become clear if you have all the details correct. You are interested in people and the world at large.

If you drew your quickie pic from the outside in . . . you are very detail-oriented and put a lot of emphasis on getting things right the first time. You can be very focused on topics that interest you. You have a high degree of self-control. You tend to hold off on letting others into your inner circle until you've had a chance to get to know them. You are also skeptical by nature and prefer the concrete and practical to the fantastical and imaginary. Others consider you to be both practical and dependable.

The Arc

On a separate piece of paper, copy the picture below, then complete it. Neatness doesn't count, so just draw it quickly, without thinking about it too much. Then turn the page to find out what your quickie pic reveals about you.

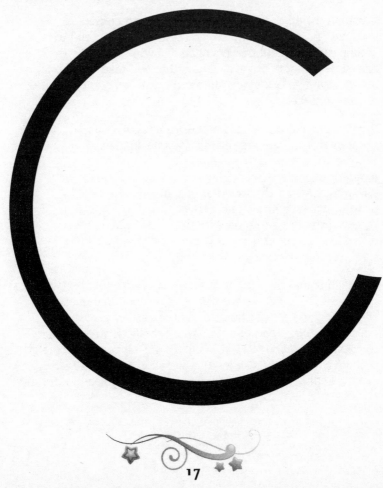

What your drawing says about you . . .

If your finished drawing is a neat, closed circle . . .
you are tidy, both in your thinking and in your
personal habits. You like the saying, "a place for
everything, and everything in its place," and try to
live by it. You are not really fond of surprises and prefer
to follow a daily routine. You value simplicity and honesty.

If your finished drawing is a sloppy, closed circle . . .
you value order and routine — in theory. But you tend to
be impatient and cut corners once in a while! You like to
experiment too, but never in ways that will take you too far
out of your comfort zone. You are trustworthy and tolerant of
others' mistakes.

**If your finished drawing is a closed, irregular shape,
not a circle . . .** you are playful and imaginative.
You like to laugh and find pleasure in
ordinary things: the sound of rain
plinking on a leaf, the sound of popcorn
poppety-popping in the microwave.
You are responsive to the needs of
others and go out of your way to make
sure everyone around you is content.

**If your finished drawing is open ended, without the two ends
connected . . .** you are something of a rebel. You question
everything and aren't afraid to ask the hard or awkward
questions others tend to avoid. Your rebellious streak may
sometimes lead you to clash with others, especially people in
authority. But it will also lead to you all kinds of interesting
places. Expect to travel widely — you're a trailblazer, after all!

Armed With Self-Knowledge

You can tell a lot about people by their body language — how they hold themselves in different situations. This quiz is best done with a friend, who can read the instructions to you when your eyes are closed. Don't forget to give her a chance to take the quiz too!

To take the quiz, begin by standing as shown, with your arms extended in front of you and your feet comfortably side by side and flat on the floor. Then close your eyes.

Have a friend read the following instructions to you (or memorize them ahead of time). Then do each task as described.

1. Imagine a helium balloon is tied by its string to your right hand. It is pulling your hand up, up, up . . .
2. Imagine that you are holding a heavy vase, full of flowers, in your left hand. It is heavy in your hand and pushing it down to the floor.
3. Picture the balloon and the vase, the balloon and the vase, each pulling and pushing on one hand, for at least 30 seconds.

When you open your eyes, where are your hands?

They are far apart. Your right arm is angled toward the ceiling, your left arm toward the floor. You are highly imaginative. Your senses are well developed, and you are in tune with both your body and your surroundings. You enjoy a rich fantasy life and can easily disappear into imaginary worlds — a thrilling novel or an entrancing video game. You can be quite passionate and are easily swayed by emotion.

They are close to where they were when you began the activity. You are logical and rational. You are not easily influenced by others. You think seeing is believing and prefer to make your own decisions based on facts, facts and more facts.

One hand has moved far from where it started, but the other is close to where it was when you began the activity. You are strongly intuitive but tend to let your logical mind overrule your gut instincts. You can sometimes be indecisive.

What's Your Secret Soul Number?

Are you a one-of-a-kind number 1? Or a mysterious number 8?

Using the chart below, add up the number value of the letters of your first, last and middle names (if you have them!). If your sum is two or more digits — for example, 125 — add those numbers together (1 + 2 + 5 = 8). You may need to do this again to get a single digit. The final one-digit figure is your secret soul number.

A=1	I=9	Q=17	Y=25
B=2	J=10	R=18	Z=26
C=3	K=11	S=19	
D=4	L=12	T=20	
E=5	M=13	U=21	
F=6	N=14	V=22	
G=7	O=15	W=23	
H=8	P=16	X=24	

What your soul number means . . .

1. **The Innovator.** You are great at coming up with new ideas and getting others to buy into them. But because you are so strong-minded, you can sometimes come across as stubborn or arrogant.

2. **The Diplomat.** You bring people together and are excellent at smoothing over troubled waters. But you can be shy and feel uncomfortable in a crowd.

3. **The Idealist.** You don't see any reason why the world shouldn't be kinder, greener, more fun. People love your enthusiasm and your energy. But others can disappoint you when they don't live up to your high standards.

4. **The Classic.** You love tradition, especially anything having to do with royalty. But that doesn't mean you can't get down and dirty — you love nature, the outdoors and animals, especially dogs and horses. But some people might find you snobby, or think you find it hard to relax.

5. **The Explorer.** You are motivated by curiosity and love to learn, learn, learn! But you tend to be impulsive and sometimes forget to look before you leap.

6. **The Romantic.** You value love and family above all else. You are deeply affected by art and music. But others may take advantage of your warm and giving nature.

7. **The Problem Solver.** You are drawn to puzzles and like nothing better than to figure out the solution. But you can be secretive and sometimes have difficulty explaining your ideas to others. Others, therefore, might see you as aloof.

8. **The Executive.** Others look up to you and value your can-do attitude, your confidence and your unfailing optimism. But you might rub people the wrong way when you barge in and take over.

9. **The Entertainer.** You are generous to a fault and will literally turn cartwheels to make others happy. You love to be the centre of attention and are a terrific storyteller and charming host. You are also highly sensitive to other people's emotions. But you may forget to pay attention to your own needs.

Crystal Magic

Different gems are said to have different magical or spiritual properties. Some bring good luck, while others protect against danger or evil. Which crystal is right for you right now?

1. What colours are you most strongly drawn to?
    a. Bright colours. > Go to question 2.
    b. Pastel colours. > Go to question 3.
    c. Dark colours. > Go to question 4.
    d. Warm colours. > Go to question 5.

2. Which shape are you most strongly drawn to?
    a. Star. > Go to question 6.
    b. Crescent moon. > Go to question 7.
    c. Diamond. > Go to question 8.

3. Are you more spiritual or more logical?
    a. Spiritual. > Go to question 9.
    b. Logical. > Go to question 10.

4. Which type of foods do you prefer?
    a. Spicy foods. > Go to question 11.
    b. Sweet foods. > Go to question 12.

5. Which appeals to you more?
    a. Fame and fortune. > Go to question 13.
    b. Peace and tranquility > Go to question 11.

6. You struggle more with . . .
    a. insecurity. > Your crystal is RUBY.
    b. frustration. > Your crystal is SAPPHIRE.

7. You aspire to . . .
    a. creative fulfillment. > Your crystal is OPAL.
    b. inner peace. > Your crystal is AMETHYST.
8. You dream of . . .
    a. love and romance. > Your crystal is EMERALD.
    b. acquiring knowledge and understanding.
    > Your crystal is QUARTZ.
9. You commonly have more . . .
    a. pleasant dreams. > Your crystal is CITRINE.
    b. nightmares. > Your crystal is JADE.
10. Which sense do you value more?
    a. Vision. > Your crystal is AGATE.
    b. Hearing. > Your crystal is QUARTZ.
11. On a bad day, you are more likely to . . .
    a. withdraw to your room and write in your journal.
    > Your crystal is ONYX.
    b. get into an argument with someone.
    > Your crystal is GARNET.
12. You tend to . . .
    a. make quick decisions and stick to them.
    > Your crystal is MOONSTONE.
    b. avoid making decisions and change your mind
    frequently. > Your crystal is SAPPHIRE.
13. You secretly crave . . .
    a. power. > Your crystal is TOPAZ.
    b. affection. > Your crystal is RUBY.

What your crystal says about you . . .

Agate is the crystal of acceptance. It encourages you to see things as they really are and has a grounding, stabilizing quality. Agate helps build self-esteem and soothes the mind and spirit. It draws people who value the real you and helps you recognize phonies or people with ulterior motives. Agate gives you courage, especially when faced with an ethical dilemma, so you can choose the correct path and stick to it.

Amethyst is the crystal of spiritual growth. It helps you connect with other people, as well as the divine. It is an excellent aid for meditation. Amethyst encourages open-heartedness, generosity and trust. It draws challenges into your life that will help you to grow into a better person. It also gives you the ability to triumph over fear and achieve your goals.

Citrine is the crystal of joy. It brings light and luck into your life. It draws prosperity and attracts friendship. Citrine will bring you abundance in all areas and help you overcome feelings of loneliness or irritation.

Emerald is the crystal of harmony. It strengthens memory, faith and hope. It promotes honesty and good communication, so it can enhance relationships with others. Emeralds can help heal a broken heart.

Garnet is the crystal of rebirth and transformation. It brings protection during periods of great change and personal growth. It offers protection, too, against nightmares and fears of all kinds. It encourages firmness of purpose and fortitude. Garnet helps boost self-confidence and can bring great prosperity and long-lasting contentment.

Jade is the crystal of wisdom. It brings peace through order and encourages simplicity, serenity and courage. Jade draws inspirational dreams and helps ward off nightmares. A powerful stone, it radiates a subtle energy that helps you find beauty in everyday life. It promotes long life and happiness.

Moonstone is the crystal of healing. It brings sensitivity to others' emotions and draws affection and kindness in return. Moonstone can help provide relief from stress and offers protection during travel. It draws feelings of comfort and belonging.

Onyx is the crystal of strength. It helps build courage in the face of adversity and protects against stress. Onyx draws stamina and encourages self-control, faithfulness and loyalty. It protects against fatigue and disappointment. Its darkness draws light into it, which improves both your outlook on life and your opportunities.

Opal is the crystal of inspiration. It stimulates ideas and imagination. It makes obstacles seem smaller, helping you avoid discouragement. Opal helps you to let go of the desire for control and to feel free and light in spirit. It helps you overcome mood swings and maintain emotional balance. Opal may increase your chances of seeing ghosts!

Quartz is the crystal of energy. It brings awakening of the spirit and invigoration of the body. It encourages clarity of thought and positive attitude. Quartz will help you focus your energy on what is truly important in life and help you achieve your goals through concentration. It can help prevent lethargy and laziness.

Ruby is the crystal of love and devotion. It brings passion and warmth into your life. It can be a protective talisman, keeping you safe in times of danger. It will help you create a happy atmosphere in your home and guard against sadness and anger.

Sapphire is the crystal of intuition and insight. It brings understanding and compassion into your life. It helps unlock creativity and self-awareness. Sapphire is an excellent aid to meditation and brings a sense of calm and delight. It can help you stave off confusion and anxiety.

Topaz is the crystal of balance. It has a calming effect and can help soothe frayed nerves and release stress. It can draw success and good fortune to you by helping you be at the right place at the right time. It can protect you from falling victim to greed or selfishness.

Are you a Lark or an Owl?

This quiz isn't for the birds: It will tell you if you are a natural morning person or someone who prefers to burn the midnight oil.

1. Sunday morning. You . . .

   a. jump out of bed and lace up your running shoes. You love to get outdoors and do something active while everyone else sleeps.

   b. roll over. Again. And again. And again. It's great to not have to go anywhere in a hurry.

   c. stretch, yawn, grab your robe and read or watch TV until breakfast time.

2. When do you prefer to do your homework?

   a. As soon as you get home from school.

   b. After dinner.

   c. In the morning.

3. Which do you prefer:

   a. A shower in the morning.

   b. A bath before bed.

   c. A shower after a sports activity.

4. Do you find it easy to get out of bed for school?

   a. It's not a problem.

   b. It depends on if I stayed up late the night before.

   c. Are you kidding? My folks need to blow me out of bed with a cannon!

5. You've been invited to a slumber party. You . . .

    a. are excited! Nothing more fun than staying up all night with your pals.

    b. are happy, but wary — you get cranky if you don't get enough sleep.

    c. reluctantly say no. You'll just wind up falling asleep earlier than everyone else and miss out on all the fun.

6. When do you feel most alert and active?

    a. Between 8 and 10 a.m.

    b. Between 10 a.m. and 2 p.m.

    c. In the evening.

7. When you go to bed . . .

    a. you like to read for a while — your parents always have to make you turn off the lights!

    b. you fall asleep as soon as your head hits the pillow.

    c. it takes you about 20 minutes to fall asleep.

8. Which would you rather see:

    a. A sunrise?

    b. A sunset?

    c. A blazing midday sun?

Scoring

1.	a1	b3	c2
2	a2	b3	c1
3.	a1	b3	c2
4.	a1	b2	c3
5.	a3	b2	c1
6.	a1	b2	c3
7.	a3	b1	c2
8.	a1	b3	c2

How you rate . . .

8-13 Lark. You're a true early bird, up with the sun. And it's working for you! You feel best when you get an early start. But by 8 p.m. it's lights out, baby! Take advantage of your larkish nature by tackling your to-do list first thing in the a.m., when your mood and energy are at their peak. Avoid starting new projects after 4 p.m. You won't retain new information as well, and your work won't be top notch if you're tiring. With this schedule, you're sure to succeed — the early bird gets the worm, after all.

14-18 Sunbird. You don't like to waste a morning sleeping in, but on the other hand, you don't need to be up at the crack of dawn either. And you like staying up late on occasion — just not too, too late; it leaves you groggy and tired the next day. Since you're at your best midday, do your homework immediately after school, when your brain is still humming. Do routine chores in the morning or early evening. With this schedule, you'll really shine!

19-24 Night owl. You're like the moonflower that blooms only at night. Or maybe a vampire. No wonder mornings are tough for you — the light! It burns! As the day goes on, you perk up more and more. By evening you're buzzing with energy! Make your night-owl nature work for you by planning ahead: Lay out your clothes for school and make your lunch in the evening, so all you have to do is grab and go in the morning. Do your homework in the early evening, when your brain is at its best. With this schedule, you're sure to be the brightest star out there.

How Observant Are You?

You will need a stopwatch or clock with a second hand to take this quiz.

Start the stopwatch (or note the time on a clock with a second hand) to begin. Then study the two sets of images below. There is only one image that is repeated in both sets. How long does it take you to find it?

How you rate . . .

30 seconds or less. Super observant! Your I-spy-with-my-little-eye talent is extraordinary. You are excellent with detail — picture yourself as a super-successful art director or international spy.

31-60 seconds. Observant. You pay careful attention to what's going on around you and notice details others might miss. Can you see yourself as a high-level corporate accountant or fine art conservationist?

60+ seconds. You're in good company. Most people take longer than 60 seconds to spot the sneaky duplicate! You can build your observation skills, though, through practice. Make a point of studying your surroundings and looking for the unusual or out-of-place objects. What you discover may surprise and delight you!

What's Your Star Sign?

Many people around the world believe that the position of the stars in the sky on the date and hour of your birth influences your personality. Find the zodiac sign that corresponds with your birthday and learn what it says about you.

♈ ♉ ♊ ♋ ♌ ♍
♎ ♏ ♐ ♑ ♒ ♓

Aries (the Ram) March 21 to April 19

You're always in motion. You learned to climb before you could crawl, and nothing scares you — even when it should! Yup, that's you zooming down the black diamond ski run, or cannonballing into the deep end of the pool while everyone else is still getting into their gear. No wonder you can sometimes be impatient or lose interest in projects that aren't 1-2-3 done.

Taurus (the Bull) April 20 to May 20

You are solid, practical, dependable — qualities that will one day make you rich, rich, rich! Taurus kids like you are great with money and terrific planners. But you also love the simple pleasures — gooey hot-fudge sundaes, shiny new toys, that comfy quilt from when you were just a baby. You ALWAYS finish what you start, and do a great job at it. Your honesty, loyalty and terrific hugs make you a great friend.

Gemini (the Twins) May 20 to June 20

You love to connect with others and you do it mostly by talking — you can talk circles around anyone! (Don't forget to take a breath now and then!) You are very intelligent; your endless curiosity and thirst for knowledge drive you to explore a wide variety of interests. They also make you a quick study when learning new skills, especially language-oriented ones like computer programming or French. You are extremely charming — funny and persuasive. But don't rely on that charm in lieu of applying good old-fashioned elbow grease — you will need to buckle down, sometimes, if you want to make your glorious dreams come true!

Cancer (the Crab) June 21 to July 22

You gravitate toward underdogs — the people and animals who need a helping hand and a warm hug. Do you always wind up bringing home stray puppies and wounded birds? (Thought so!) Home is very important for you: you love your own space and spend a lot of time and energy on making it a cozy retreat. You would happily spend all weekend sewing pretty purple curtains for your bedroom. You're also very sensitive and can take a long time to recover from perceived slights.

Leo (the Lion) July 23 to August 22

Leos are the royalty of the zodiac — and happiest when their subjects give them the royal treatment they deserve! You are naturally bossy, but people go along with your plans because you are so much fun to be around. When all is right in your world, you are warm-hearted, generous and full of great ideas. But when you feel frustrated or ignored, you turn into a beast!

Virgo (the Virgin) August 23 to September 22

When you were a toddler, you kept all your toys
neat and organized. And NO ONE ELSE COULD
TOUCH THEM. You still like things organized
and are excellent at any task that involves lots
of details or keeping track of schedules. You have a tendency
toward shyness, but when you can get past that nervousness,
you are warm-hearted and excel at looking after other people.
You are also great at fixing things — like repairing that broken
spring on an old toy, or coming up with a workaround for a
computer bug. Because you are a perfectionist, you can be
overly self-critical. Get plenty of exercise to help keep your
tendency toward self-doubt at bay.

Libra (the Scales) September 23 to October 22

Libras are the peacemakers of the zodiac. You
see both sides of any issue and do your best to
help bring other people together. You do this by
making other people feel good — you have much natural charm.
You are also very artistic and are drawn to all things beautiful —
dance, painting, fashion. You tend to be very social and are at
your best around other people. But you can be fickle, and your
desire to please others means you sometimes make promises
you can't keep. You have difficulty speaking up for yourself and
must remember not to give in or give up too quickly.

Scorpio (the Scorpion) October 23 to November 21

Like the scorpion this star sign is named for,
Scorpios are to be respected. Smart, strong-willed
and intense, you can be dangerous when poked! You
tend to be somewhat introverted, with a long memory
and a sharp mind that's terrific at solving puzzles or outsmarting

others in strategy games like chess or Battleship. You also tend to be secretive and don't trust others easily. But when you let them into your life, you can be the most loyal and supportive friend ever!

Sagittarius (the Archer) November 22 to December 21

Everyone loves to have fun, but no one more than the Sagittarius girl. You love people, all of them, and tend to have lots of friends. You also love sports and games of all kind — you'll always say yes to any sport, whether it's field hockey or tiddlywinks! You tend to be bold, honest and independent — a combination that sometimes leads others to think you need to learn some of Libra's skills in diplomacy. Almost nothing gets you down.

Capricorn (the Goat) December 22 to January 19

You are serious and very mature — with a settled approach to life that keeps you well grounded. No wonder grown-ups turn to you for help with routine tasks — you're the perfect class monitor or most in-demand babysitter in town! You can be very ambitious and are very good at making your dreams a reality. Yet your favourite things involve the simple pleasures — traditional holiday celebrations are right at the top of your list. Remember it's ok to be silly sometimes. Even though you're mature for your age, you're still a kid!

Aquarius (the Water Bearer) January 20 to February 18

Aquarians are the eccentrics of the zodiac. You love to be different: You like to dress in kooky clothes, listen to unusual music, tell jokes that no one else seems to get. You tend to

be dramatic and very spontaneous — things happen when you walk into a room (but no one can predict what it will be!). Since you are easily bored, you turn inward to make your own entertainment. You can be very creative and will excel in technology or the arts if you are given free rein to express yourself.

Pisces (the Fish) February 19 to March 20

You are a dreamer. Your magical inner world is much more appealing than the ho-hum routines of everyday life. As a result, you tend to retreat into it whenever you can, especially if you are going through a tough time at home or school. You also tend to be very sensitive, with a natural desire to reach out to people who seem sad or lonely. Together, these qualities make you highly creative. Pisces kids often grow up to be gifted musicians or artists. They also frequently lose stuff — because they are more focused on their inner worlds than the here and now.

Picture This!

Study the sets of pictures below. Think about how each group makes you feel. On a separate piece of paper, jot down a few words (three to six) that sum up your feelings about each group of animals. Find out what your answers reveal about you.

1.

2.

3.

What your feelings say about you . . .

1. **This set of pictures relates to your early childhood.** If you used positive words, you were happy. If you used negative words, you may have had a sad or difficult start in life.

2. **This set of pictures relates to your enemies.** If you used positive words, you have few or no enemies. You feel safe and comfortable at home and school. If you used negative words, you feel as if you have enemies. You frequently have your guard up.

3. **This set of pictures relates to people you look up to.** If you used positive words, you admire and respect people in authority and think they can help you achieve your own goals. If you used negative words, you tend to distrust people in authority and think you will have great difficulty in achieving your goals in life. The specific words you chose reveal character traits you dislike in yourself and others.

The Strangest Journey

The questions in this quiz are open-ended. There are no right or wrong answers. Just answer with what feels natural to you. Your answers will reveal secrets about your nature.

1. Imagine you can pick one place, any place, anywhere in the universe, to live for the rest of your life. Where is it?
2. You are lost in the desert. You are hungry and thirsty. You have almost given up hope when a village comes into view. You blink and notice that in the opposite direction, an oasis lies on the horizon. Which way do you go?
3. Snow day! How will you spend your unplanned free day?
4. Your home is in flames. You have the chance to grab just one thing before the firefighters scoop you to safety. What do you save from the fire?

What your choices say about you . . .

1. This question reveals how content you are with your life.

♦ **If you chose the place where you live now,** you are generally content with your life.

♦ **If you chose a distant or exotic destination for your new home,** you are restless and eager for a change. Others might consider you to be something of a dreamer or a romantic.

♦ **If you can't decide where you'd like to live,** you are a free spirit, without many attachments to others. No one would ever call you sentimental!

2. This question reveals your attitudes toward work and play.

♦ **If you chose to head for the oasis,** you put pleasure and fun ahead of work. You tend to procrastinate and have trouble sticking to one task at a time. You can be impulsive and get annoyed under restrictive rules.

♦ **If you chose to head for the village,** you put work ahead of play. You're a take-charge kind of gal who takes deadlines seriously and likes nothing better than successfully completing a project.

♦ **If you chose any other option,** your attitude toward work depends very much on what that work is! If it's a project you care about, you'll work day and night without a break. But if you have no interest in the task? YAWN.

3. This question reveals your attitudes toward money.

◆ **If you chose to spend the day hanging out at home,** then you tend to be a saver. Your piggy bank is too stuffed to oink!

◆ **If you chose to spend the day shopping,** you are the kind of gal for whom money is easy come, easy go. If you have it, you spend it!

◆ **If you chose to spend the day engaged in a sport,** you like to spend a little and save a little. You never know when that nest egg will come in handy!

◆ **If you chose to hang out with friends,** then you are generous with your money when you have it but also sensible. You think about each purchase you make very carefully to decide if it will give you long-lasting value.

4. This question reveals what you value most.

◆ **If you chose to save a photo album, or other item of sentimental value,** you value family and friendship.

◆ **If you chose a robe, or other item of clothing to cover yourself up,** you value your health and personal safety.

◆ **If you chose jewellery, a wallet or anything else that's worth a lot of money,** you value material things.

◆ **If you chose your phone or computer,** you value practicality and common sense.

What Act of Nature Are You?

1. You bombed your spelling test! You . . .
   a. rip up the offending test and toss it in the nearest trash can. > Go to question 2.
   b. cry and complain to your friends that the test was unfair. > Go to question 3.
   c. hide the test in the bottom of your backpack and don't tell anyone about it. Ever. > Go to question 4.
   d. explode! > Go to question 5.

2. Your sister borrowed your sweater without asking! You . . .
   a. make her take it off — right now! > Go to question 9.
   b. borrow her favourite sweater tomorrow without asking. > Go to question 10.
   c. make a huge stink in front of her friends. They need to know what a sneak she is! > Go to question 6.
3. You've just watched a super-sad movie. You . . .
   a. can't stop crying! > Go to question 6.
   b. get all choked up and go off to hug your stuffie for comfort. > Go to question 7.
   c. whine and moan about how bad the movie was — you hate downer movies like that! > Go to question 8.

4. Your former best friend is telling lies about you. You . . .

    a. seethe. > You are an AVALANCHE.

    b. confront her at recess and ask her to stop. > Go to question 6.

    c. keep your head down — you don't want to call any more attention to yourself now. > You are a BLIZZARD.

5. You've been knitting a scarf for forever. You almost have it finished when your dog gets a hold of it and tears it to shreds! You . . .

    a. slam every door in the house.
    > You are an EARTHQUAKE.

    b. go quiet. Scarily quiet.
    > You are a VOLCANO.

6. Your arch-rival just got the part you wanted in the school play! You . . .

    a. bravely congratulate her, then go home and have a good cry. > You are a TSUNAMI.

    b. demand another tryout. > You are a HURRICANE.

7. You enjoy nothing better than . . .

    a. a good gossip session with your pals. > You are a BLIZZARD.

    b. a good belly laugh. > You are an AVALANCHE.

    c. a good argument. > Go to question 5.

8. You tend to . . .

    a. keep your feelings to yourself. > You are a BLIZZARD.

    b. share your heart with everyone. > You are a TSUNAMI.

    c. share your feelings with your closest friends. > You are an AVALANCHE.

9. Which animal appeals to you most?
    a. Tasmanian devil. > You are a HURRICANE.
    b. Fire-breathing dragon. > You are a VOLCANO.
    c. Dolphin. > Go to question 6.
10. Your favourite team has just won the Stanley Cup! You . . .
    a. throw your popcorn bowl in the air as you whoop and shout! > You are an EARTHQUAKE.
    b. breathe a sigh of relief. > You are a BLIZZARD.

What your act of nature says about you . . .

Avalanche. You may look calm and cool on the outside, but on the inside you're an accident waiting to happen — for someone else! You bide your time, waiting for the perfect moment to strike. And when you do, watch out world, 'cause not even the abominable snowman can stop you when you're on a roll. Your favourite food: An ice cream sandwich.

Blizzard. You can be quite a cool customer and sure know how to make others shiver in their boots. Your secret weapon: The cold shoulder.

Earthquake. You like to shake things up. You tend to make mountains out of molehills. Your unpredictable nature — sweet one second, raging the next — can make others tremble. Your favourite food: Milkshakes.

Hurricane. Your temper is huge, huger, hugest! But that doesn't stop people from wanting to hang out with you. They enjoy your enormous energy and air of excitement. Your secret weapon: You are long-winded.

Tsunami. You are usually calm, but when you lose your temper, nothing survives your wrath! You dissolve in tears easily. You like to make a clean sweep of things. Your secret desire: Wavy hair.

Volcano. When you get angry, you seethe. And then you blow your top! You sometimes wind up spewing out harsh words you may regret. Remember not to burn bridges and just to go with the flow. Your secret weapon: Your explosive temper.

What's Your Chinese Astrological Sign?

Check the chart below to find the animal symbol that corresponds to your year of birth. Then find out what each animal represents and what it reveals about you!

Rat. You are ambitious and very imaginative. You can be very charming, but when things don't go your way you can turn on people and become manipulative or vengeful.

Ox. You are a born leader who likes doing things your own way and who will always succeed through hard work and perseverance. You are faithful and loyal, but sometimes impatient with a tendency to sulk.

Tiger. You are enthusiastic and optimistic. Nothing gets you down. You are extremely courageous and know you have the strength and confidence to achieve your goals.

Rabbit. You are fun to be around. Some people think you are fluffy — without much depth — but they're wrong. You are intuitive and thoughtful and have excellent taste. You love fashion and anything pleasant or beautiful.

Dragon. Dragons are the stars of the Chinese zodiac. You are larger than life, with a giant-sized ego and a giant-sized heart to go with it. Dragons love to be the centre of attention and can be very demanding. But you are also exciting to be around, highly capable and very popular!

Snake. You are a very private person and like to act quietly, behind the scenes, rather than in the full glare of the spotlight. You think deeply, and when you feel like it's time for a change, you can easily shuck off old habits and friendships and start over again with a seemingly brand-new identity.

Horse. You think with your heart before your head. You can therefore be impulsive. Luckily, your enormous capacity for hard work allows you to correct mistakes quickly and effectively. Passionate, lively and fun to be around, horses make good friends and colleagues. You are good with words and can be something of a chatterbox!

Sheep. You tend to be tender-hearted, with a simple openness that others find refreshing and appealing. You enjoy making things beautiful and comfortable, and taking care of others. You also enjoy your own comfort and can be whiny if things aren't to your satisfaction.

Monkey. You have a magnetic personality. People are drawn to you for your playfulness, imagination and cleverness. You love to chat, which can sometimes annoy others when you won't yield the floor to them. Luckily, your excellent sense of humour helps keep relationships with others sweet. You have such a wide range of interests, you may have difficulty sticking to one thing.

Rooster. You are open, honest and direct. You love bright, shiny things and beautiful clothes. You can be hot tempered, and your feathers are easily ruffled if people don't treat you with respect.

Dog. You are not just man's best friend, you're everyone's best friend — loyal, honest, trustworthy and extremely affectionate. You can be plagued with self-doubt, though, and tend to worry about every little thing. You are easily hurt and tend to hold a grudge.

Boar. You are calm, frank and thoughtful, sensitive to the moods and needs of others. Although you have a short temper, you hate quarrelling and do everything you can to keep the peace. Most of the time, you are moderate in your habits, tolerant and open-minded. But if you get pushed to the breaking point, watch out! You secretly crave a life of luxury.

This Little Piggy

To take this quiz, you'll need a separate piece of paper and a pencil. There are no questions. Instead, you will perform a simple task: Draw a picture of a pig. NOTE: Artistic talent is not important in this activity.

When you have finished your picture, read on to find out what your piggy pic says about you.

What your drawing says about you . . .

1. Where did you draw your pig?

   Top of the page. You are a born optimist, with a very positive attitude toward life.

   Middle of the page. You have a very realistic attitude toward life.

   Bottom of the page. You are naturally pessimistic, with the expectation that whatever can go wrong, will.

2. Which direction is your pig facing?

   To the left. You believe in traditional values. You are great at remembering the birthdays of all your friends and family members.

   To the right. You are an innovator. You have a terrible memory for dates and are not big on traditional holidays or celebrations.

   Facing you. You are honest, direct and a bit pig headed.

   Facing away from you. You frequently find yourself the butt of many jokes.

3. Did you draw your pig with many details (5 or more features beyond basic body parts)?

   Yes. You tend to be distrustful of others and very cool and logical in your approach to life.

   No. You are a risk taker. You are highly emotional. Some people may consider you naïve or overly trusting.

4. How many legs are visible in your picture?

   All 4 legs. You are not easily swayed by the opinions of others.

   Fewer than 4 legs. You are either somewhat insecure or going through a period of great change in your life.

   More than 4 legs. You have a great sense of humour.

5. What kind of ears does your pig have?

   Big. You are a good listener (the bigger, the better!).

   Small and neat. You listen to your own heart.

   No ears. You can be closed-minded.

6. Did you draw a tail?

   Yes. You always finish what you start and value a job well done.

   No. You dislike wearing your hair in braids.

The Writing on the Wall

Whether your penmanship is picture-perfect or an all-over-the-page scrawl, it reveals secrets about you. Each dotted I and loopy L reveals something about your personality. On a separate piece of unlined paper, copy the text below — a selection from J. M. Barrie's *Peter and Wendy* — then read on to find out what your handwriting says about you.

The last sounds Peter heard before he was quite alone were the mermaids retiring one by one to their bedchambers under the sea. He was too far away to hear their doors shut; but every door in the coral caves where they live rings a tiny bell when it opens or closes (as in the nicest houses on the mainland) and he heard the bells.

What your handwriting says about you . . .

Take a look at the letters in your handwriting sample and answer these questions.

1. How big are your letters?

    Large (7 mm or greater). You are outgoing and get along well with all kinds of people.

    Medium (4-6 mm). You value accuracy and keeping cool under fire. You are very logical.

    Small (2-3 mm). You have excellent attention for detail and are very observant. You are a planner, with a good sense of humour and sharp intellect. You can be secretive and distrustful of others.

Very small (2 mm). You believe rules should be followed at all times. You are impatient with others, especially those who are attention-seekers.

2. Does the letter size get bigger or smaller?
   Bigger. You are trustworthy and very trusting of others.
   Smaller. You are cautious and can be deceitful.

3. Which way do your letters lean?
   Slightly to the left. You tend to be somewhat reserved in nature.
   Heavily to the left. You hide or suppress your emotions and can be moody. You like to be the centre of attention.
   They go straight up and down. You have good control over your emotions. You make wise decisions after considerable thought.
   Slightly to the right. You are artistic in temperament. You are good at reading other people's emotions. You enjoy good conversations with others.
   Heavily to the right. You sometimes have trouble controlling your emotions. You express yourself clearly, loudly and often. You are prone to overreacting.

4. What shape are your letters?
   Rounded. You like to please others and avoid confrontation.

Pointy. You like to learn new things. You are also ambitious. The higher the peaks and the pointier your letters, the more ambitious you are.

5 Are your letters connected to each other?
Connected to each other. You are systematic and orderly.
Open at the bottom. You listen to and follow your heart. .

6. How widely are your letters spaced?
Relatively wide. You are independent and don't like to be crowded.
Relatively narrow. You prefer to spend time with others rather than alone.

7. What do the looped letters look like?
Narrow. You may be feeling tense.
You tend to be skeptical of others' motivations.
Very wide. You are relaxed and spontaneous.
You enjoy trying new things.

8. How did you dot your Is?
Right over the body of the I. You mean what you say and say what you mean.
High above the body of the I. You have a terrific imagination.
To the left of the I. You are a procrastinator.
To the right of the I. You are always in a hurry.
Drawn at an angle. You are overly self-critical and impatient.
Circles. You are a visionary and a romantic.
No dot at all. You are independent and a big picture kind of person.

9. How did you cross your Ts?
   At the very top. You are ambitious and optimistic, with high self-esteem.
   Right in the middle. You feel comfortable in your own skin.
   With a long line. You are determined and sometimes stubborn.
   With a short line. You are impatient and a bit lazy.
10. Are your Os open or closed?
   Open. You are very talkative and tend to share your feelings easily.
   Closed. You are quiet and tend to keep your feelings to yourself.
11. How much pressure did you use in writing your sample?
   Heavy pressure. You take life seriously and honour commitments.
   Light pressure. You have a great deal of empathy.

Heavy pressure

Light pressure

Are You Actually a Mermaid?

1. Your bedroom tends to smell like . . .
   a. lilacs.
   b. Limburger cheese.
   c. lingcod.
2. You are exceptionally fond of . . .
   a. coral jewellery.
   b. glitter and sparkles.
   c. headbands.
3. There is a puddle on the sidewalk. You . . .
   a. step over it.
   b. walk around it.
   c. splash through it!
4. Which tongue twister is easiest for you to say?
   a. Rubber baby buggy bumpers.
   b. She sells seashells by the seashore.
   c. A cheap ship trip.

5. You secretly love the name . . .
   a. Ariel.
   b. Shellie.
   c. Bob.
6. You prefer to take . . .
   a. long walks in the country.
   b. bubble baths.
   c. pictures.

7. Your ideal vacation would be . . .
   a. scuba diving in the Seychelles.
   b. Paris, dahling!
   c. mountain climbing.
8. How long can you hold your breath? (Try it!)
   a. 15 seconds or less.
   b. 16-40 seconds.
   c. 41+ seconds.
9. It's your birthday! How do you celebrate?
   a. Have a party at an all-you-can-eat sushi bar.
   b. Pool party!
   c. Slumber party at the museum.
10. Do you have a tail?
   a. Yes. Doesn't everyone?
   b. No . . . not yet, anyway.
   c. I'm not telling ;)

Scoring

1.	a2	b1	c3
2.	a3	b2	c1
3.	a1	b2	c3
4.	a1	b3	c2
5.	a3	b2	c1
6.	a1	b3	c2
7.	a3	b2	c1
8.	a1	b2	c3
9.	a2	b3	c1
10.	a3	b1	c2

Your mermaid rating . . .

10-16 Landlubber. Don't feel too crabby. Though your chances of being an actual mermaid are slim, you have serious fairy princess potential. Invest in a good-quality magic wand.

17-22 Mer-maybe. Are those fish scales on your lower body, or just frightfully dry skin? Take swimming lessons pronto.

23-30. Fish out of water. You are SUCH a mermaid! You are constantly combing seaweed out of your hair, and your breath smells like clam chowder. Toes are overrated, aren't they?

Are You a Thinker or a Doer?

Do you plan out the action, or put the plan into action?

1. You've been given a new school assignment — you have to create a diorama or video about the Vikings' arrival in Canada. You . . .

   a. grab a shoebox, paper and some clay. You can't wait to get started on your diorama!

   b. take a stack of books out of the library. You'll need plenty of research materials to figure out how those Vikings lived, worked and played.

   c. check out a few websites, then start making a list of shots you'll need for your video.

2. You've signed up for the school play! Which job will you go for?

   a. The star, of course!

   b. The playwright.

   c. The stage manager.

3. You're making scrambled eggs with your sister when — *EEEK!* — the pan catches on fire! What do you do?

   a. Call for help.

   b. Smother it with baking soda.

   c. Tell your sister what she has to do to put the fire out.

4. Which game do you prefer?

   a. Mousetrap.

   b. Chess or backgammon.

   c. Dodge ball.

5. Which would you prefer?

   a. Listen to your favourite band on high-quality, noise-cancelling headphones.

   b. Go to a concert by your favourite band.

   c. Be in a band, playing keyboard or drums.

6. You've joined an after-school softball league. What position do you want to play?

   a. Pitcher — everything depends on you!

   b. Catcher — you are in the thick of the action, and you get to call the pitches.

   c. Right fielder — you're safely out of the main action, but still a player.

7. *Brrrrrr!* It's frosty out! How do you choose to spend your day?

   a. Read a fave book or try to level up in your fave video game.

   b. Grab skis, skates or a toboggan to make the most of the day.

   c. Bake cookies and heat up some yummy hot chocolate.

8. What is your favourite subject at school?

   a. Gym or art.

   b. French or science.

   c. Math or English.

Scoring

1.	a3	b1	c2
2.	a3	b1	c2
3.	a2	b3	c1
4.	a2	b1	c3
5.	a1	b2	c3
6.	a3	b2	c1
7.	a1	b3	c2
8.	a3	b2	c1

How you rate . . .

8-12 Thinker. You spend a lot of time in your head thinking about all kinds of things. You are imaginative and curious, and you love to learn. You enjoy strategy games and activities that require you to solve problems or come up with new ideas. You tend to be cautious in new situations. Take a risk! You might enjoy branching out.

13-18 Think-a-do. You are flexible and are very good at adapting to new situations of all kinds. Sometimes you prefer to sit back and observe — that's a great way to learn, isn't it? At other times, though, you are swept with enthusiasm and jump right in! You enjoy a healthy range of activities and can be equally happy experimenting with a new set of coloured markers at home or taking a hike by a mountain stream.

19-24 Definitely a doer. You get antsy even thinking about sitting still! You love movement and prefer to be doing something active every single moment. You love to get in there and get dirty, whether it's playing football with your pals or growing colourful mould on stale bread as a science experiment. You tend to be impatient and don't read instructions carefully

enough. This can get you in hot water! Count to 10 before you start something new — this will give your brain a chance to catch up with your body and save you some oopses in the future.

Picture This 2

Study the sets of pictures below. Think about how each group makes you feel. On a separate piece of paper, jot down a few words (three to six) that sum up your feelings about each group of animals. Then read on to find out what your answers reveal about you.

1.

2.

3.

What your feelings say about you . . .

1. **This set of pictures relates to how you view tricksters or troublemakers.** If you used positive words, you may be something of a troublemaker yourself! If you used negative words, you tend to place high value on following rules and sticking to routines.

2. **This set of pictures relates to your teachers.** If you used positive words, you have good relationships with your teachers and enjoy learning from them. If you used negative words, you haven't always had the best relationships with your teachers. School sometimes feels like quite a challenge for you!

3. **This set of pictures relates to your friends and friendships.** If you used positive words, you have many good friends and are a good friend. If you used negative words, you tend to be a more private person. You have just a few, but very close, friends.

How Do Others See You?

1. What's your favourite time of day?
   a. Morning.
   b. Afternoon or early evening.
   c. Late at night.

2. You tend to walk . . .
   a. fast with long steps.
   b. fast with small steps.
   c. medium speed, alert and looking around you.
   d. slowly, looking down.
   e. very slowly.

3. You're talking to a group of people. You tend to . . .
   a. stand with your arms folded across your chest.
   b. stand with your hands clasped together.
   c. stand with either one or both hands on your hips.
   d. stand close to whomever you are speaking to and touch them often as you speak.
   e. fiddle with your hair, touch your face or straighten your clothes.

4. It's been a long day and you finally get a chance to relax. How do you like to sit?
   a. With your knees bent and your legs neatly aligned side by side.
   b. Cross legged.
   c. With your legs stretched out or straight.
   d. With one leg curled under you.

5. You've just heard a hilarious joke! How do you react?

   a. A big, over-the-top, appreciative laugh.

   b. A plain old ordinary laugh.

   c. A quiet chuckle.

   d. A shy smile.

6. It's party time! How do you enter the room?

   a. You make a loud, showy entrance — you like to be noticed.

   b. You enter quietly and immediately look around for a familiar face.

   c. You slip into the room and hope no one notices you.

7. You're hard at work on a project. Your brother interrupts you — again! How do you feel?

   a. You welcome the break — you've been working so hard!

   b. You feel extremely irritated — why can't people just leave you alone?

   c. You go back and forth between welcoming the interruption and being irritated by it.

8. Which colours do you prefer?

   a. Red, hot pink or orange.

   b. Black.

   c. Yellow or green.

   d. Purple or blue.

   e. Brown or grey.

9. What's your favourite position to fall asleep in?

   a. Stretched out flat on your back.

   b. Face down on your stomach.

   c. On your side, curled into a ball.

   d. On your side, head resting on one arm.

   e. Head completely under the covers.

10. Which dream do you have most often?
    a. That you're falling.
    b. That you're fighting or struggling with someone.
    c. That you are searching for something or someone.
    d. That you're flying or floating.
    e. You usually don't have dreams.

Scoring

1. a3	b5	c10		
2. a5	b4	c3	d2	e1
3. a5	b4	c3	d2	e1
4. a2	b3	c8	d5	
5. a10	b8	c4	d2	
6. a10	b5	c2		
7. a5	b2	c8		
8. a8	b10	c3	d6	e1
9. a6	b3	c4	d2	e1
10. a5	b8	c3	d4	e2

How you rate . . .

70-80 Solar flare. Others see you as both strong and strong-willed, with a take-charge, leave-no-prisoners personality. Many admire you for your self-confidence and straight-talking. But you may put others off — they may think you are self-centred and too bossy.

55-69 Supernova. Others see you as exciting and adventurous. They consider you to be a natural leader and enjoy being in your company. People think you're a really good sport and that you'll pitch in when it's time to do the work, whatever it is.

43-55 Moonlight. Others see you as open, considerate and charming. You are viewed as a good friend and a good team player who will always be there for others. You are also considered to be very practical — a can-do kind of gal who can be relied upon.

34-42 Starlight. Others see you as sensible, thoughtful and sensitive. They think you are sometimes too modest about your abilities and talents. You are considered to be very loyal and trustworthy, a quiet but respected member of the team.

25-33 Shooting star. Others see you as careful, thorough and detail-oriented. Because of your cautious nature, people know you can be relied on for good advice. Some people might consider you to be shy or timid and unlikely to try new things.

17-24 Firefly. Others see you as shy and somewhat nervous. People do not expect you to take the lead on anything, but rather to wait for others to ask you to take part. Some people might also see you as indecisive and lacking confidence.

What's Your Spirit Animal?

Many First Nations peoples believe that each of us has a spirit animal, or totem, that represents a mixture of key personality traits. Totems can be associated with a particular tribe or family, or can come into your life as a spiritual guide in times of need. Use the chart below to find your spirit animal. Start with the date you were born. If it's a two-digit number — for example, 23 for May 23 — add those numbers together (2 + 3 = 5). You may need to do this again to get a one-digit figure. In the chart below, start counting from left to right. Cross off the animal you land on when you get to your number. Repeat this until there is only one animal left in the chart. That is your spirit animal.

Otter	Wolf	Hawk	Elk
Eagle	Salmon	Cougar	Owl
Raven	Snake	Horse	Bear

Otter

Otters are full of fun! You can be very creative but also logical. You seek truth in all things.

Wolf

Wolves love freedom above all else. You tend to take the lead in most things. You can be very trusting and very generous. Your feelings run deep.

Hawk

You possess deep insight and can be a true visionary. You are a free thinker and value your independence but crave acceptance by others. You can be impulsive at times.

Elk

Pride is your strength and your downfall. You command respect and admiration. You are a hard worker who values achievement and monetary reward. You can be ornery if challenged.

Eagle

You are the observer. You combine creativity with accurate intuition. You are determined, strong-willed and athletic. You are motivated by idealism.

Salmon

You are motivated by a desire for harmony in all things. You can be very generous and giving and will sacrifice your own desires to please others. You value the comforts of home. You tend to be moody.

Cougar

Determination is your greatest strength. You seek to lead a life full of meaning and purpose. You are ambitious and tend to dominate others. You can also be exceedingly gracious and charmingly spontaneous.

Owl

You have an eye for detail. A perfectionist, you can sometimes be short-tempered with others. You are articulate, clever and can keep a secret. You rise to a challenge and almost always succeed when you put your mind to it.

Raven

You are very spiritual. You use every tool you can — charm, wit, diplomacy, humour — to make your ideals come true. You value community and strive for peaceful relationships. You have an air of mystery that others find intriguing.

Snake

You are intense and introspective, concerned with personal growth and transformation. You enjoy praise and seek it out. You can be secretive and have difficulty trusting others. You can achieve great things.

Horse

You have tremendous stamina and can overcome any hardship to achieve success. You get along with others. You are honest, kind and understanding. You have a very curious nature.

Bear

You are fiercely protective of your family and friends. You are adaptable and patient but can take swift action when the occasion demands it. You tend to keep your thoughts and feelings to yourself.

Made to Order?

Are you the baby of the family, spoiled by everyone else? Or the bossy big sis? Maybe you're a middle kid, trying to get noticed, or a confident only child.

Take this quiz and find out if your answers match your real-life birth order or reveals a more surprising inner nature!

1. Which description fits you best?
   a. Outgoing.
   b. Peacemaker.
   c. Perfectionist.
   d. Mature for your age.
2. Two of your best friends are having an argument. What do you do?
   a. Try to get them to make up.
   b. Stay out of it. It has nothing to do with you.
   c. Tell them to get over it. They're making a big deal about nothing!
   d. Wind up right in the thick of it. You can't help getting involved!
3. Dinner time! You . . .
   a. call everyone to the table.
   b. sit down and wait to be served.
   c. set the table.
   d. offer to help serve.

4. What does your desk look like?
   a. A total disaster!
   b. Perfectly organized, of course.
   c. Covered with photos of friends, family and pets.
   d. Relatively tidy and functional.
5. Which job would you prefer?
   a. Raking leaves.
   b. Babysitting.
   c. Delivering community newspapers.
   d. Job? No thank you!
6. Your hockey team has organized a bake sale to raise money. What do you do?

   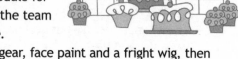

   a. Put together a schedule for when each member of the team will staff the sale table.
   b. Dress up in hockey gear, face paint and a fright wig, then call out "bake sale today!" to everyone who passes by.
   c. Quietly let your coach know you can do any job she needs done.
   d. Bake 12 dozen cookies with your pals.
7. It's your great aunt Tillie's birthday party! At the dinner table, you find yourself squished between your great uncle Bill and Tillie's best friend, Jamilla. What do you do?
   a. Tell Bill and Jamilla all about yourself — your friends, your school, your favourite sport, your pet tarantula.
   b. Listen respectfully to Bill and Jamilla's tales about when they were kids.
   c. Plot your escape — ASAP!
   d. Chat politely, then get up and help clear the table.

Scoring

1.	a1	b2	c3	d4
2.	a2	b4	c3	d1
3.	a3	b1	c4	d2
4.	a1	b4	c2	d3
5.	a2	b3	c4	d1
6.	a3	b1	c4	d2
7.	a3	b2	c1	d4

How you rate . . .

7-12 Are you a youngest child? Babies of the family tend to be charming, outgoing and attention seeking. They can be rebellious and can throw temper tantrums if they don't get their way. Youngests tend to be the life of the party and are generous and tolerant of others. They prefer to let others make decisions.

13-18 Are you a middle child? Middles tend to be sensitive to the needs of others but sometimes have difficulty expressing their own feelings and desires. Middles make great friends, great diplomats and great business executives. They crave appreciation.

19-23 Are you an oldest child? Oldests love to take charge. Why not, when they are so good at it! Oldests have very high standards and value doing things right the first time. They love to feel needed and take pleasure in a perfectly made bed, or to-do lists with all the dos checked off. They are very responsible.

24-28 Are you an only child? Only children brim with self-confidence and self-esteem. They enjoy the company of older people, sometimes more than that of their peers. They tend to be very responsible and reliable. When they see something that needs to be done, they quietly take charge and do it without fuss or bother. Only children know they are special, so they don't need to seek attention and have very little patience for those who act out or act badly.

The Wheel of Fortune

Does good fortune rain down upon you? Or are you always the one getting splashed as the bus (the one you missed) pulls away from the curb?

1. You have an important test today. Your alarm failed to go off. What next?

    a. You arrive at school after the test has started. But you ace it anyway.

    b. You arrive at school after the test is over and the teacher gives you a zero.

    c. Your friend's mom just happens to pass by and gives you a lift to school. You arrive right in time to ace the test.

    d. You wake up before the alarm is supposed to go off. You get to school on time and take the test. No probs.

2. You are walking down the street with your BFF. What next?

    a. A kid whizzes by on a skateboard and knocks your books to the ground.

    b. A kid whizzes by on a skateboard and knocks your books to the ground, into a puddle of mud.

    c. A kid whizzes by on a skateboard. You realize it's your long-lost cousin. Love fest!

    d. You arrive home without incident.

3. You are playing backgammon. You need to roll a 4 and a 3 to win. Any other combination and you are sure to lose. What happens next?

    a. You roll a 4 and a 3. You win the game.

    b. You roll a 4 and a 2. Your opponent wins on her next turn.

c.   You roll double 6s, which don't help you much, even though they are normally the best roll.

d.   You roll a 1 and a 2. On her next turn, your opponent gets an even worse roll. You roll again and win the game!

4. You've put your name in the hat for a chance to win two tickets for your favourite band. What next?

a.   Your best friend wins the tickets. She takes you as her guest!

b.   Your name is drawn first!

c.   You don't expect much . . . and you're right. You don't get to go to the concert.

d.   Your name isn't drawn. You invite your friends over for a karaoke sleepover and give your own concert at home.

5. How many bones have your broken in your life?

a.   One.

b.   More than one.

c.   None.

d.   Too many to count!

6. Your best friend has a nasty cold. She accidentally sneezes all over you! What next?

a.   You bring her some cookies to cheer her up, slip on the stairs to her apartment and sprain your ankle. Then catch the cold to boot.

b.   Catch the cold, of course.

c.   You make her your grandma's special lemon-ginger tea. She beats that cold.

d.   You get the sniffles but fight them off with Grandma's special tea.

7. Your soup Thermos leaked in your backpack! What next?

a. The soup ruins the book report you spent all week on. Your gym clothes, too, so you miss out on a fun session of dodge ball. And now you have no lunch.

b. The soup only drips a little. No harm done.

c. The soup soaks your homework assignment, but you dry it out and turn it in on time.

d. Nothing is damaged except the backpack!

8. You've entered your poem called "Down with Ducks" in a writing contest. What happens?

a. You win! And the prize is $100!

b. You win! The prize is a nice plaque.

c. You come in second. The prize is $10.

d. You get an honourable mention. Along with every other person who entered the contest.

9. A dragon has come to your town. What next?

a. The dragon decides you look tasty. Chomp!

b. The dragon is lonely. It befriends you.

c. The dragon eats your family but spits you out.

d. The dragon turns out to be a fairy in disguise. She turns you into a dragon!

10. You believe that . . .

a. you make your own luck.

b. lucky charms and lucky numbers can totally save you from disaster!

c. everybody has some good days and some bad days.

d. other people get all the luck.

Scoring

1.	a2	b1	c3	d4
2.	a2	b1	c4	d3
3.	a4	b1	c2	d3
4.	a3	b4	c1	d2
5.	a3	b2	c4	d1
6.	a1	b2	c4	d3
7.	a1	b4	c3	d2
8.	a4	b2	c3	d1
9.	a1	b4	c3	d2
10.	a4	b2	c3	d1

How you rate . . .

10-15 Out of luck. It seems like things never go your way! Improve your chances by planning ahead and paying attention to what's going on around you. A little preparation = a lot of success!

16-25 Roll again! You haven't always had the best luck, but you know that Lady Luck is fickle and your fortunes can change like that — *SNAP!* Keep an optimistic attitude and watch your step — that dark spot on the sidewalk might just be a $100 bill!

26-35 Lucky duck. Wow! You've been on a real lucky streak! Maybe that's because you know how to make your own luck — seeing the silver lining in every opportunity and knowing how to shake disappointments off.

36-40 Lady Luck herself. Keep rolling lucky 7s and coming up a winner in every situation? How do you do it? Maybe it's your positive, can-do attitude. Maybe you work hard so rewards follow. Or maybe you've swallowed a seriously lucky horseshoe.

The Imaginary Journey

This quiz will take you on an imaginary journey. Write your answers to each question on a separate piece of paper. Then turn the page to find out what your answers reveal about the true you.

1. An alarm clock rings. You wake up and discover you are not in your own room. Even though you do not recognize it, the room is oddly familiar. Describe the room, including what the furniture is like and how the room is decorated. Make sure to describe how the room makes you feel.
2. You know it is time to get up and go outside. Do you want to leave or would you prefer to stay in the room?
3. You get up and go outside. You start walking. You realize you are heading toward the seashore. As you walk, how many people can you see?
4. How far away are the people?

What your journey says about you . . .

1. The room represents your life today. If you described the room as comfortable and pleasant, it means you are satisfied with your life. If the room was uncomfortable or unpleasant, it means you are dissatisfied with your life. The details you gave when describing your room relate to how you feel about the past. If your room is stuffed with furniture, you sometimes live in the past. If your room is bare and spare, you prefer to live in the present.

2. If you want to get up and leave the room, you are eager to grow up and embark on the next stage of your life. If you want to stay in the room, you prefer not to rush into the next stage of your life, but to keep things as they are for now.

3. Questions 3 and 4 have to do with how you relate to the people around you. The more people you see, the more extroverted you are. If you see a large crowd, you tend to feel energized in the company of people — the more the merrier! If you didn't see any people, you enjoy spending long periods of time on your own — crowds tend to drain you.

   Most people see one or two people on the beach. If this is you, you are most comfortable in smaller groups. You enjoy socializing with others, as well as quiet time on your own.

4. If the people you saw were quite close to you, you tend to talk more than you listen! If the people were far away, you tend to be somewhat reserved and listen more than you talk.

Are You Psychic?

1. The phone rings. You . . .
   a. almost always know who it is.
   b. pick up the phone without looking and say into it, "Mom, I texted you an hour ago — I left the laundry bucket in the laundry room."
   c. see that it's your friend Hannah — OMG you were just thinking about her!

2. Your BFF gives you a funny look across the lunchroom. You . . .
   a. know EXACTLY what she is thinking!
   b. wonder what's going on . . .
   c. nod and send her a telepathic message back: "Yes, I'll meet you in the library in five."

3. You are doing a math activity using a pair of dice. You have to roll the dice 100 times. You concentrate hard on the dice and . . .
   a. roll lucky 7 — seven times in a row!
   b. roll combinations perfectly in line with probability — and get 100 percent on the worksheet.
   c. seem to roll an exceptionally high percentage of 1s — spooky!

4. You've lost your keys. You close your  eyes and picture them in your mind. You . . .

   a. now know exactly where they are.

   b. spend the next 45 minutes looking for them and then discover them still hanging in the keyhole!

   c. hold out your hand and — *VOOP!* — they appear in your palm.

5. You dreamed about a plane crash last night. This morning . . .

   a. you discovered that a plane crashed last night!

   b. you ate toaster waffles with maple syrup. They were delish.

   c. you got a call from a friend who's just found out her family's going to Florida on vacation! You advised her NOT to take that trip!

6. When you look at people, you . . .

   a. see colours — auras! — shimmering around their heads.

   b. can see their futures playing out like a soundless video before your eyes. That's why you rarely look people in the eye.

   c. can almost always tell what they are feeling.

7. You find a necklace slipped between the pages of a library book. You take it in your hand and . . .
   a. wonder who left it there.
   b. instantly know who the owner is.
   c. feel a connection to the owner.
8. You sometimes get flashes in which you . . .
   a. know what's going to happen next.
   b. feel like you've experienced this moment before.
   c. have no idea what's going on, like you've been transported to another world.
9. You believe in . . .
   a. ghosts – because you've seen them.
   b. ghosts – because you are afraid of them.
   c. the Tooth Fairy – because she brings you money.
10. People say you are . . .
    a. logical and down to earth.
    b. spiritual and intuitive.
    c. open-minded and curious.

Scoring

1.	a1	b3	c2
2.	a2	b1	c3
3.	a3	b1	c2
4.	a2	b1	c3
5.	a2	b1	c3
6.	a2	b3	c1
7.	a1	b3	c2
8.	a3	b2	c1
9.	a3	b2	c1
10.	a1	b3	c2

How you rate . . .

10-18 I See . . . You are not psychic. You don't seem to have any special talent for clairvoyance or telepathy. That's fine with you since you think it's all bunk anyway.

19-25 Your future is cloudy. You may possess some psychic powers. But then again, it could just be heartburn. You can sometimes read people's minds, especially your BFF's! Does that mean you are psychic or just super in sync with her? Either way, it's easy to predict your gift for empathy will win you many friends and much success in life.

26-30 Psychic to the stars. There's something going on here . . . you know things before they happen, can move objects with your mind and see straight into other people's souls. Use your powers for good.

Which heavenly Body Are you?

1. Which do you value most?
   a. Brains. > Go to question 2.
   b. Fame. > Go to question 3.
   c. Loyalty. > Go to question 4.

2. You consider yourself . . .
   a. fairly knowledgeable about the stars and planets. > Go to question 5.
   b. a real astronomy buff! > Go to question 6.
   c. more interested in what's here on earth. > Go to question 7.

3. You would prefer to win . . .
   a. a golden spoon in a cooking contest. > Go to question 8.
   b. first place in a popularity contest. > Go to question 9.
   c. a green ribbon for environmentalism. > Go to question 10

4. What's your plan for the future?
   a. I have a five-year plan and will stick to it. > Go to question 11.
   b. I make plans but frequently change them. > Go to question 12.
   c. I live in the moment.   Go to question 17.
   d. I let other people do the planning for me. > Go to question 13.

5. How would you describe yourself?
    a. Mysterious. > You are URANUS.
    b. Bright. > Go to question 15.
    c. Distant. > Go to question 16.
    d. Friendly. > You are EARTH.

6. What's your favourite fashion accessory?
    a. A pretty headband. > You are SATURN.
    b. A cool belt. > Go to question 17.
    c. A filmy scarf or veil. > You are VENUS.
    d. A sunny smile. You are the SUN.
7. Which do you think about most?
    a. The past, present and future. > You are the MOON.
    b. Lunch. > You are EARTH.

8. What's your favourite flavour of ice cream?
    a. Something traditional, like chocolate or vanilla. > You are the MOON.
    b. Something exotic, like salted caramel. > Go to question 9.
9. You prefer to have:
    a. A large circle of friends. > You are SATURN.
    b. A few, very close, very loyal pals. > You are VENUS.
10. Which pattern would you prefer for your bedsheets?
    a. Camouflage. > You are EARTH.
    b. Stars and unicorns. > You are the MOON.
11. Which sport appeals to you more?
    a. Mountain climbing. > You are the SUN.
    b. Spelunking (caving). > Got to question 13.

12. Winter or summer?

    a. Winter. > You are PLUTO.

    b. Summer. > You are VENUS.

    c. Neither! > Go to question 14.

13. Friends describe you as . . .

    a. one cool customer! > You are PLUTO.

    b. totally grounded. > You are EARTH.

14. Dogs or cats?

    a. Cats. > You are VENUS.

    b. Dogs. > You are PLUTO.

15. Which would you prefer?

    a. Being the Hollywood director. > You are the SUN.

    b. Being the Hollywood star. > You are SATURN.

16. Which pattern do you prefer for your clothing?

    a. Solids. > You are URANUS.

    b. Stripes. > You are SATURN.

17. Your favourite animal is a . . .

    a. dog. > You are PLUTO.

    b. mythical animal, like a unicorn. > You are a SHOOTING STAR.

What your heavenly body says about you . . .

Earth. You are well grounded. You enjoy gardening, riding a dirt bike and making mud pies. You are not afraid to get your hands dirty.

Moon. You are a gentle, loving person. You have a magnetic personality and exert a powerful influence over others. You may actually be made out of cheese.

Pluto. You are fun loving and a bit eccentric, with a bark that's worse than your bite.

Saturn. You are gracious and charming. You can be vain. You like jewellery, especially rings. You are somewhat distant and reserved with strangers. You secretly think jokes about Uranus are hilarious.

Shooting star. You attract attention wherever you go. You dazzle others with your wit. You sometimes emit a powerful tailwind.

Sun. You are an attention hog. Me! Me! ME! Naturally, you deserve all that adulation. You are so bright, so unique, a real star. Make sure you shut off the lights when you leave the room.

Uranus. You are a natural comedian. Your favourite line is, "But seriously, folks!" You enjoy making arm farts and telling knock-knock jokes. You secretly wish Neptune weren't quite so boring.

Venus. People think you are mysterious, but you are merely confused. You sometimes feel suffocated.

Your Inner Landscape

To take this quiz, you will need a separate piece of paper and a pencil.

There are no questions. Instead, you will draw a landscape with a few items in it.

NOTE: Artistic talent is not important in this activity.

When you have finished your picture, turn the page to find out what it reveals about you.

1. First, draw a house.

2. Next, draw a ladder.

3. Next, draw a horse.

4. Now draw a storm over your scene.

5. Finally, add some flowers to your scene.

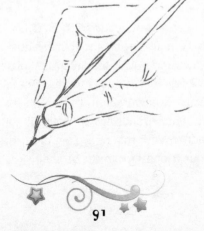

What your drawing says about you . . .

1. **The house represents you.** If you have drawn a
    neat, comfortable-looking home, it means you
    see yourself as a strong, warm person. If the
    house looks crooked or incomplete, it means
    you have doubts about yourself.

2. **Is the house big and close to the viewer, or small and far
    away?** If the house is large, it means you have a high degree
    of self-knowledge. If it is smaller, it means you are still not
    sure about who you are and what your true desires are.

3. **Did you draw windows on the house?** If so, is there
    anything visible through the windows? (Did you draw
    curtains? A pot of flowers, or a face?) If so, it means you are
    open and honest, and do not put on a false face for others.
    As a result you are a terrible liar, so honesty is not just
    the best policy, it's the only policy for you! If there are no
    windows on your house, or you cannot see inside the house,
    it means you protect yourself and only open up to people
    who have earned your trust.

4. **Did you draw a chimney?** If so, it means you are
    good at keeping secrets.

5. **The ladder represents your friends.** If it's leaning
    up against the house, it means your friends depend
    on you. If the ladder isn't touching the house, that
    means you keep your friends at a distance. If the
    ladder is brightly coloured or drawn with thick,
    strong lines, your friendships are solid. If you drew
    a wiggly ladder, with thin or broken lines, then
    some of your friendships might be shaky.

6. **The horse represents your family.** If the horse is close to the house, you feel close to your family. If it is far away, you would like a better relationship with someone in your family. If your horse is tied to a post or wearing a saddle, it means you want to have more control over your own life. If the horse is free, you feel like your family lets you make your own choices as much as possible. If the horse is eating, you are content and satisfied and feel safe within your family circle.

7. **The storm represents an obstacle you may be facing.** If the storm is huge, dark and threatening, it means you are currently dealing with hardship. If the storm is small, distant and relatively mild, it means your life is calm and trouble free at the moment.

8. **The flowers represent your hopes and dreams.** If you drew many large flowers, you are optimistic about the future. If you drew flowers in full bloom, you will achieve your goals sooner rather than later. If you drew the flowers close to the base of the house and under or around the ladder, your friends and family will support you in your dreams. If you drew flowers in window boxes on the house, you will achieve your dreams mostly through your own efforts. If you drew more than one kind of flower, then you have many interests and find it difficult to decide what path to follow in life. If you drew one kind of flower, you are focused on one goal and will do everything it takes to achieve success in that field.

Head vs Heart

Do you let logic guide your decisions, or do you rely on gut feelings to get where you're going? Answer always, sometimes or never to each of the following statementts to find out your decision-making style.

1. You are spontaneous and tend to go with the flow.
2. You hate, hate, HATE making plans! You never stick to them anyway.
3. When you meet someone new, you instantly decide if you like them or not.
4. You feel like you have a special purpose in life — if only you knew what it was!
5. You consider yourself to be creative, a real artsy type.
6. You tend to be a worrier.
7. You make to-do lists but find it hard to stick to them.
8. You are good at spotting a liar.
9. When you have to make a decision, you prefer to sleep on it. You'll wake up knowing exactly what to do!
10. When putting something together, like a beading craft, you prefer to just figure it out as you go, rather than follow the instructions.
11. You find it easier to remember faces than names.
12. You speak with your hands.
13. You remember many of your dreams.
14. When you hear someone speaking, you tend to respond more to their tone of voice than their words.
15. You like to read or study lying down.

Scoring

Give yourself 3 points for each always, 2 points for each sometimes and 1 point for each never.

How you rate . . .

15-24 Engineer. You are more logical than intuitive. You take a step-by-step approach to decision making and value facts over emotions. You are very practical and dislike drama. People value you for being level-headed.

25-35 Business executive. You use both your brain and your heart to make decisions. You know that feelings count, and it is important to consider more than just the cold hard facts when making a decision. You can't always explain why you made a decision, but you generally feel confident with your choices. People value you for your flexibility and good sense.

36-45 Artist. You are more intuitive than logical. You rely on your instincts and emotions to guide your path through life. You are very creative and dislike being tied down by schedules, rules or rigid plans. People value you for your empathy.

Look for these other great quiz books!